Rain's Realm:

The Future In Bloom

RainBlue

DEDICATION

I dedicate this book to America and the World for a better life of peace and Love now and forever more.

CONTENTS

ACKNOWLEDGMENTS

Thank-you! Just thank-you to
Life, our forefathers,
elders; everyone past and
present. Life isn't always
easy, but it is awesome! I'm
very happy to be alive at
this time to write this book
and hope it helps as it is
intended to:)

Also, thank-you to my adult
kids for their patience with
me and help with technology:)
It is because of their help
that I am able to bring this
to you much faster. I love
them all greatly and am so
proud of them:)

1 INTRODUCTION

I have thought a lot about how to start this book and organize it! I have sought guidance from Above as well as many people. This book will never be truly done, but I hope to put the most important ideas in it to me. Maybe others will make my ideas even better? Maybe they won't? Please keep in mind I write this with the most loving of intentions:)

I look back through history and see loving intentions murdered by power and hate:(I hope and pray that does NOT happen to the ideas here! I believe Love is given freely. Love does NOT force others to do what it wants. Love makes requests, suggestions, and gives guidance. It is up to each of us to decide to follow or accept Love and by to what measure.

Power and force are NOT Love! I believe all laws should support Life and come from Love.

They should be enforced with Love as well. By this, I mean with compassion, understanding, patience, kindness, and wisdom.

Also to understand this writing, you may need to know some of my main beliefs? I will put many of them through-out the book and why. However, I will plainly state them here:

I believe in a Supreme Being (God, Godess, Godness, Allah, Whomever/However you label such Supreme Being) that rules the Universe for Good. This Supreme Being is Almighty, Alpowerful, and All Loving. I call the Supreme Being God. I also believe God is Love and Light as told to us many times by Jesus.

I believe the "Sacred Books" are to be Honored, but NOT above God. They are books of history and guidance- just as this book may be. Some of you just got angry with me, but if you keep reading, I'll explain myself! I can't quote the "Sacred Books" specifically.

However, they all say many times, "God is the same yesterday, today, and forever more." If this is true and knowing the Bible best myself, He sent prophets, dream interpreters, apostles, and disciples to write the Bible. Would He also not send these types of people today? Was Muhammad one of them sent in his time? Which leads me to an observation.

We all go through different times of our lives. Some times are more loving than others! Sometimes as we age and our minds may forget, we are also not as nice or loving. So if after I write this with Love and hope to make the world a better place for all generations into the future, I write something not so Loving; throw it away! Do NOT follow it or force anyone else to do so either! Remember what I said about power and force as well as Love:)

I believe in the Constitution of the United States of America:) The

Constitution was highly
debated by our Forefathers!
They debated whether mankind
was basically good or evil.
Basically good being that
given choices of right and
wrong, we would usually pick
what was right, good, and/or
loving. If we were evil, we
would choose wrong most of
the time. We would seek
power and control over
others. We would force
people to be or do things
they felt were wrong. They
decided some people choose to
do wrong, but that most
people were GOOD:)

It is that basic decision
the Constitution was written
on! They realized
Government, Kings, and
Churches sought to control
the people. They realized
some control was needed.
That some laws protected the
people. However, some laws
did not as I already
mentioned. This is why they
built in a checks and balance
system of government. A
tiered system of power
distribution. Therefore, no
one branch of government

could take full power and force over the People! For if this started to happen or happened, the GOVERNMENT and NOT the Constitution was to be changed BY THE PEOPLE! There is, however, a way to change the Constitution described within it too. I have ideas on some changes to the Constitution that ultimately will peacefully and Lovingly change our government. That's one of the main reasons for this book:)

Another main reason is to see if the People would vote me in as Senator in Michigan to go to Washington DC and work to make these changes myself. Since this will be first published in 2015, maybe the People would want me to be President instead? If put in office, I would continue voicing problems and solutions to everyone as I have begun to do here. Regardless, I will continue voicing problems and solutions and hope the world will be a better place for many, many generations...dare

I say forever?...because I
write and share this with
you:)

2 CONSTITUTIONAL CHANGES

Amendment 28: Congress shall pass no law exempting itself or the public; all laws apply to EVERYONE equally.

Or alternately as described in my "TV Idea" later in this book:

Amendment 28: Congress shall pass no domestic law without a 65% majority vote of "We the People" and may not if passed by said vote exempt themselves.

Amendment 29: All budget changes must be approved "By the People" during a scheduled vote of the People- ie- The first Tuesday in November every two years. In a true emergency, the House of Representatives may make a TEMPORARY change to provide relief to the People of the United States ONLY- not a foreign country.

Amendment 30: The budget will be a "pie system" based on percentages to be adjusted as prescribed in Amendment 29 and can never be more than 100%. If something is adjusted up then something must be adjusted down. If finances or a "piece" is added, all pieces are adjusted down equally to account for the new "piece". (The basic starting pie to be described later in this book and why.)

Amendment 31: Congress shall pass no law without first posting online and in print the full, accurate, and truthful text of said law for thirty (30) days.

For thirty days, "We the People" read, debate, and vote on the law. Each person gets one vote. Votes are given to the constituents' Representatives in Congress.

For one week, Congress takes the vote tallies and debate points brought up by "We the People" to the floor of Congress as previously prescribed. NO changes can be made to the proposed posted law or the process begins again and the previous posting, debate, and vote is

deleted entirely! On the
seventh day at 3:00PM EDT,
Congressional debate ends and
Congressional voting begins
taking into account the
debate points and votes of
"We the People". Voting ends
after all of Congress votes.

All Congressional votes
are counted and the law
passes or fails as previously
posted. Congressional votes
and proceedings are recorded
as previously prescribed as
well.

Amend Amendment 16 to end
the income tax and all other
taxes and create a Federal
Sales Tax as described later
in this book. The amount
established or changes to the
amount would be subject to
previous Amendments. It
would be prudent to have a
firm beginning amount. I
have therefore chosen the
amount that has been talked
of often in the last many
election cycles. Also, the
Federal Sales Tax would be
implemented as further
explained later in this book.

Amendment 16 if amended would
then be:

>Amendment 16: For means
>of operation, Congress
>establishes a 17% Federal
>Sales Tax on all goods
>and services bought or
>sold in or from the
>United States of America
>with the exemption of
>food and products for
>daily living.

3 ECONOMICS: Business Model, Budget, & Taxes

If you've paid any attention to Congress since 2010, you know they cannot pass a budget. Yet the House of Representatives is responsible for doing so as per the Constitution. I proposed my Amendments to fix not only this constant fighting and upheaval, but to propose another business model as well.

When President Obama ran for office in 2008, one of his "promises" was "No more Wall Street on the backs of Main Street". Well, he has failed to keep that promise. In fact, it seems that Wall Street is on our backs even more. CEO pay is still way more than the average worker's pay! The reason for this is it's suppose to indicate the "health" of the company. The more the CEO gets paid, the "healthier", more profitable the company is suppose to be. This is not always true. Proof would be the bailouts of 2008.

What if the "health" of the company was determined by how much the average worker was paid, benefits provided to everyone in the company, and bonuses paid? What if owners received 20% of the company's profits while management received 20% of the remaining 80%? However, the management 20% would be divided equally among all managers.

Let's use a very scaled down example. A company has five managers. They make a $100 profit for the month after overhead, benefits, and hourly wages are paid. The owner gets $20 for the month. Management splits 20% of the remaining $80 which would be $16. Management would make 10% higher wages than other workers to start with. So the five managers in this example would get an extra $3.20 each for the month. This leaves $64 for other workers to split evenly. Say our example company has 25 other workers- 5 each per manager. This would give

each worker a bonus of $2.56
for the month.

Some of a company's
monthly profits come from a
Federal Sales Tax if
Amendment 16 is amended which
we will believe it is for the
purposes of this book. I
will explain this more soon.
This has also been called a
Consumption Tax here in the
United States and a VAT or
Value Added Tax in European
Countries. This added amount
will help make companies
"healthier" as well. So by
my example, to make the most
of this new business model,
unless the owner puts in
regular work hours as a
manager, they would not get
an hourly wage. They would
be more inclined to seek
greater profits to share at
the end of the month!

Managers and other
workers would set up
household budgets based on
their hourly wages. Your
budget should never be more
than you make. This is
called "living within your
means". Government, mainly

Congress and the President(s) need to learn this! Higher hourly wages in a company means a "healthier" company also.

Anyway, budgeted correctly, a "healthier" company makes financially "healthier" workers. It probably makes happier workers too which would lead to happier, healthier communities, families, etc. It has a ripple effect. Remember, my example was extremely scaled down for easier understanding! By the example, a worker's family would be able to buy another bottle of shampoo, shaving cream, or other products at a dollar store. Those workers would then likely get better bonuses too! One dollar also buys a bag of rice or 32 oz. box of pasta which means you can feed your family more. (Those prices are here in Michigan anyway.)

Even with this scaled down version, I'm able to show you the greater monthly benefit. Imagine the greater benefit in truth of thousands of "unbudgeted" dollars per year! I would suggest budgeting your "unbudgeted" dollars as well. Save some, give some, and spend some. I suggest what you save be broken down for other larger goals like greater retirement savings, a marvelous vacation, shore up emergency savings, raise college savings, or all of the above.

TAXES

Before I get into the Government's "pie budget", I want to cover where the money for the pie comes from. We would end State Sales Tax, income, property, and estate taxes as well as any other taxes I may not know of. We might have to do this slowly over time, but not any slower than a couple of years. This will be explained more later. However, all these taxes would be replaced with a 17% Federal Sales/Consumption Tax. It would be set-up this way.

NO tax on food, toilet paper, household cleaners,

laundry soaps, and personal cleaners-products used by most families and individuals for day to day living. Some of these items are currently in the States' Sales Taxes. That would end! Everything else would be taxed when purchased. This includes business to business sales including internet purchases.

The business selling goods charges the tax. The business buying goods pays it. In this way, corporations will be paying taxes too! It adds considerably to the pie. Since tourism is a multi-billion dollar industry here in the United States, even tourists would help the country's financial situation.

At this time, I would like to explain a rule change for the banking industry as it provides part of the government pie. Instead of charging interest on loans, banks will charge the 17% Federal Sales Tax and spread it out over the life of the

loan like they do with
interest now. Each month
banks send an accounting
report to the House of
Representatives who maintains
basic budgeting and financial
responsibility enforcing the
United States' budget.

The report will state the
amount of tax for loans, new
loans (short term and long
term loans broken down), and
loans to end in the next
month. The House of
Representatives uses these
totals as the basis of their
budget. The main pie if you
will. In this way, the House
of Representatives always
knows ahead of time the least
amount of money they have for
the next month. The 17%
Federal Sales Tax from all
other places and purchases
makes the pie bigger.

Before I finish
explaining the banking
changes, I need to explain
how the new Federal Sales Tax
would be implemented. The
17% Federal Sales Tax would
be a "pass-up" situation.
Individuals would no longer

need to keep track of taxes or file taxes! Clutter of tax files for past years could be thrown out after final income tax years have expired. Individuals would only need to concern themselves with knowing they could cover the sales tax at purchase or the payment if in a loan.

In my experience, not only would our houses be more clutter free, but we would be more stress free! Again, less stress leads to healthier, happier people and families. Businesses and government entities would be responsible for the paperwork. Their paperwork would be much easier too! They would keep track of the sales tax they have collected each month. Then they would keep 90% of it and pass-up 10% to the next taxing authority.

For example: Here in Michigan, the next taxing authority would or could be a city, township, or village. The city, township, or village would then total the passed-up amounts. They keep 90% of that total and pass-up 10% again to the next taxing authority.

This same keep 90% and pass-up 10% after totaling passed-up amounts continues all the way up to the House of Representatives for the pie budget. So to continue the Michigan example as a list:
Businesses
City, Township, or
   Village
Counties
State
Federal (House of
   Representatives)

Now that you know how the Federal Sales Tax would be implemented, I will finish explaining the banking changes. The banks are the exception to the pass-up rule as they will pass-up 80%. Of the 20% the bank keeps, 10% of monthly tax earnings would be divided among customers' savings accounts. This must be stated on the House of Representative's accounting report as well. Again, banks report 100% of the Federal Sales Tax in monthly payments, but show the accounting break down to the House of Representatives as previously explained. The final total on the page is the budget total. Banks also keep 10% to pay their employees.

The House of Representatives then totals all bank totals, subtracts all ending bank totals for the next month, and informs all departments of the next month's basic budgets. Each department which is a "piece of the pie" then uses that basis with the previous month's bonus to make their budgets for the following month. The House of Representatives should also inform the departments if they are looking at any bigger cuts or differences due to expiring long-term loans. This should encourage responsible lending and establish a check and balance system with local, state, and federal governments.

BUDGET

The beginning, basic
budget would be 10% to
government wages, 20% to
military/defense, 10% to
Social Security, 10% to pay
off the National Debt, 10%
saved- disaster relief fund,
20% to welfare programs or as
I like to think of them as
prosperity programs (health,
food, shelter) for US
Citizens, 10% divided among
foreign countries' treaties
or agreements, and 10% back
to the states equally to
shore up their budgets if
needed or for special
projects. Sending 10% back
equally to the states helps
the less touristy states and
the smaller states. Yet it
still rewards the other
states. The more prosperous
each state is the more
prosperous we, The United
States of America, will be as
a whole!

4 FORECLOSURE & BANKRUPTCY

I spoke some earlier about no more interest for mortgages by replacing it with the Federal Sales Tax. Well, now I'd like to write about some other bank and credit changes. Before I do, however, I want to leave my greater generalization and timelessness to expose some truth about the latest "housing debacle". The "housing debacle" of about 2002-2010. The one that really hit in 2007-2009. I wish to explain this to help you understand why I would make the bank and credit changes I write about. Also, I feel it's important to know the truth so it doesn't happen again in the event no changes occur.

I am using my personal experience with this! Back in November 2000, my daughters and I came to the Upper Peninsula on a plan made with my then husband to buy a house that he and the boys would move into with us the following June at the latest. He closed on the house with me in February 2001. However, forty-two days later he filed for divorce. I should not have trusted my lawyer and looked out for myself more during the divorce, but I didn't. I was ordered to refinance the house in the divorce "if offered a viable, suitable loan". Well, the refinance loan was viable for the first two years in my case. Mortgage and refinance loans were also viable in the cases of many others.

You see, the public has been told that many people took out loans they could NOT afford. This is NOT true! They took out PERFECT loans for the first two or three years! Since my loan was one of the 2/28's, I was told by my lender as many others were, "If you pay all payments on time for the first two years, you can refi again into a thirty year fixed loan near the end of the two years."

The banks and mortgage companies were offering both 2/28's and 3/27's by the time any government action was taken to stop them. The mortgage company I closed the refinance with said they would be the ones to refinance me again in two years. I paid on time even though I was injured two weeks after closing on the refinance and haven't worked much since.

However, as you might have guessed, they did NOT refinance me again at the end of two years. Instead, my monthly interest doubled and almost tripled in the next six months! My payments went from about $750/month to almost $1,000/month at the two year mark and almost $1,600/month at the two and a half year mark.

This is where part of the Libor Scandal comes in. These 2/28's and 3/27's meant that the interest rate was fixed for the first two or three years. After the first two or three years, the

interest became an ARM
(Adjustable Rate Mortgage).
The ARM's were based on the
Libor rate with the first
adjustment made on the loans'
anniversary and every six
months thereafter. So in
truth, the banks and mortgage
companies could have just
left all loans on the FIXED
rate. I believe the reason
they didn't was for evil
intent!

Please let me explain!
Most of the states where
these types of loans were
taken out had local
governments that were and
maybe still are dependent on
property taxes. When houses
went into foreclosure, many
local governments lost their
income. Maybe not all of
their income, but a very
large amount. The houses
sold well under assessed
value causing assessments to
be adjusted down. This is
what led to the "under water"
loans part of the "housing
debacle". In fact, one city
that was hit very hard by
this we as a nation are still
paying for in 2014- DETROIT,

MI! Of course, Detroit had other corrupt government officials too.

Once the houses were foreclosed on, many sat empty. Empty houses often become infested, moldy, or otherwise in disrepair. This again lowered property values and local government income. The banks and mortgage companies used the "housing debacle" or more appropriately named "mortgage debacle" to take down local governments.

If local governments go down, the State's Government is bound to be affected too! Had the banks and mortgage companies not wanted to take down governments, all they had to do was let people stay on their FIXED loans. I believe, but can't prove, that the Federal Government knew about all of this and wanted it to happen as well. Congress wanted the public more dependent on them. One last point I'd like to make about this seems kind of random. The point is that rents have skyrocketed and not come back down!

By now you're probably wondering about the foreclosure and bankruptcy changes I would make? I think you can better understand the interest replacement with the Federal Sales Tax now too? I would end foreclosure! I would also end bankruptcy as it is currently. Bankruptcy today is equal to stealing in my opinion. A person has used credit, promised to pay later, and now files bankruptcy to not pay at all. Some people just got into financial trouble due to sudden job loss, injury, or illness. Unfortunately, many people make a habit out of bankruptcy. My changes seek to provide relief for those in need and stop the habit cycle.

All foreclosures and bankruptcies must go to court and be heard by a judge. Let's rename foreclosure, bankruptcy to "Financial Adjustment Cases". A

Financial Adjustment Case can be filed by the lender, the one who owes payment, or both. Once filed, ALL bills owed must be listed and turned into the court before the hearing. When the case is filed, there will be an immediate freeze of credit reported to all three credit bureaus- Transunion, Experian, and Equifax. The court will use the person's name, address, and social security number or names and numbers if married to report the freeze. The freeze remains until all bills listed are paid in full. Only a person's or couple's debit card, checks, or cash can be used to pay- no credit!

There is to be no more Debtor's Jail either. If after the Financial Adjustment is ordered the debtor doesn't willingly pay or for some other reason can't properly handle their own finances, the court can order direct pay- like a garnishment. However, if a person quits work so as not

to pay or tries to "play the
system" in any way then the
case could be noted for the
judge to review. If this
sort of review needs done,
the judge may make
adjustments again or order
the warrant for arrest at the
judge's discretion. The
point is, you said you'd pay
and now you will no matter
how long it takes. Maybe
knowing this, people will be
more careful with their
finances from the beginning?

5 CAMPAIGN & ELECTION REFORM

The Constitution allows states to decide how officials are elected at both the state and federal levels. However, I believe states should only decide how state officials are elected. Federal officials should be elected per a uniform campaign and election. Meaning, the rules are the same for every state! I propose the following idea for the Federal Officials of the President with the Vice President, Senate, and House of Representatives.

Currently, the FEC (Federal Election Commission) has over-sight of the campaigns and funds. If you want to run for office, you fill-out one of their forms and give it to them. Then every quarter you also report donations made to your campaign to the FEC and how those funds were used. I would keep the registering with the FEC to run for President with the Vice President, US Senate, and US

House of Representatives. I would also keep the FEC as over-seers of funding with changes as to how donations are made. I will explain these separately beginning with donating and funding.

To donate and fund campaigns, we would stop all direct donations! Instead of donating to the candidates, we would donate to a campaign "pool" fund at the FEC. When anyone, including corporations, makes a donation, they would say which donation "pool" fund they are donating to.

Let's say I decide to send $30 to the FEC. I enclose a note that says I want $10 to go into the Presidential "pool", $10 to go into the Senatorial "pool", and $10 to go into the House of Representatives' "pool". The FEC would then put $10 on each "pool's" accounting books or sheets. The FEC would also be responsible for distributing these funds appropriately. I will explain this distribution and use with campaign, election reform next.

My ideas for campaign and election reform are the following. All people who want to run for one of the Federal Offices as defined earlier would be required to register with the FEC by January 20th or if the 20th falls on the weekend then by the following Monday at 5:00PM local standard time. The FEC would then total candidates and "pools". The FEC would reserve or save back half of each "pool". Then they would distribute the other half of the "pool" equally among the candidates on February 1st or if the 1st falls on a weekend then the first Monday following February 1st. The candidates use those funds to run their campaigns from February 1st to the first Tuesday of May.

On the first Tuesday of May, there would be an elimination vote. The ten candidates with the most votes go on until the final vote and election on the 1st Tuesday of November. The top ten would equally divide up the reserved "pool". These funds would be released on June 1st or the following Monday if the 1st is on a weekend. Also, the FEC would continue collecting donations and dividing them equally among the ten candidates in each "pool" to be distributed on the 1st of each month thereafter or the Monday following the 1st if on a weekend. ie: July, August, September, October, and November. Once voting is complete in November, the FEC makes no further distributions until four years later when the election year begins again for the President or two years later for US Senators and US House of Representatives who are up for election or re-election.

Candidates would report to the FEC how the funds were used. The FEC could post said reports on their website. I recommend it because then "We the People" can be more informed about the candidates we will be voting for. Myself, I would prefer someone who stretched their dollars best! That candidate would more likely do the same with the budget.

There would be no more early voting. Voters would have until the 1st Tuesday of October to request a mail-in absentee ballot with a copy of their photo ID. This could be a driver's license or a state issued ID. If a driver's license, proof of citizenship must also have been given to acquire it. Another alternative would be congress makes a law, that is passes a Bill or an Act ordering the States to issue FREE photo voter IDs. The states are also allowed to make required laws on registering to vote. When you go register to vote, they could take your picture and mail the ID to you.

Absentee Ballots must be filled out and post-marked no later than the 1st Tuesday of November to be counted. Moreover, students away at

college could "transfer"
their vote from their home
area to their college area.
They also could still vote by
absentee ballot instead of
the "transfer". However,
they would need to choose by
the 1st Tuesday of October.

Back to campaigning. As
a law forcing the media to do
the candidates a "favor"
would be unconstitutional, I
would suggest that they film
a five minute video of each
candidate talking preferably
about changes they would like
to make or solutions to
problems. Tell us what they
would do if we voted them
into office. These five
minute videos would be played
like a commercial at the top
or bottom of each hour on a
rotating basis. I would also
suggest this be done FREE for
the good of our country.
However, they need to make
money too. Therefore, I
would encourage them to
charge a nominal fee. The
fee would be the same for all
candidates. The rest of a
candidate's campaign strategy
would be up to them.

Over the past fifteen years or so there has been a government push to put kids into school at younger and younger ages. If not school then daycare that is more of a pre-school. I believe this is wrong for many reasons. The Main reason is an issue of bonding which psychiatrists insist is important! Psychiatrists say it's important for mental and emotional health through-out our lives. Ultimately, it affects our physical health as well.

Another reason is that it leads more to what I call the "Bonk-Bonk Theory". There are too many kids and not enough adults per kid. The kids are more able to "take over" and misbehave or be unruly. Then there's always a health issue because the more people are put into groups and the larger these groups are the more illnesses there are to pass around. It also gets passed around faster! The following idea

to change our education
system addresses these
issues.

I propose we keep kids
"homeschooled" at least until
sixth grade. I would like to
open a conversation about the
middle school years as well
as maybe have some studies
done or previous studies
noted to decide how to teach
the middle school years. I
would be inclined to change
our education of
"homeschooling" through
eighth grade. You probably
noticed I put homeschooling
in quotes? It's because I
propose to have a modified
homeschool system. Please
don't be so upset you stop
reading because I am sure my
ideas will strengthen
families and communities!

So for now, we will
consider the modified
homeschooling for children
through fifth grade. This,
as you know, is traditionally
considered the elementary
school grades. The
traditional starting age has
been five or six years old

and would technically continue to be so. As a child nears five or six years old, his or her parents would decide if they want to homeschool or "homeschool". I believe most of you are familiar with homeschooling.

I have homeschooled all four of my children at one time or another. My boys were in public school at first, homeschooled, and went back to public school. My daughters were homeschooled first and went to public school second. I went to head-start (4 years old- now known in most schools as Pre-K)and public school all the way through. It is this experience with the joys and problems of both that I came up with what I believe is a better way, a modified homeschool system. So for my example, the parents choose to "homeschool". (Well, I wouldn't have this part of my book if they didn't! LOL)

The "homeschool" would be a partnership with the public school. Instead of continuing to use the quotes, let's rename the modified "homeschool" system to partner(ed) homeschool. As parents decide to partner homeschool, they contact the Superintendent, Principal, or assigned Partner Homeschool Administrator. At first, this contact would have a questionnaire for parents to answer. Later, but before the start of next year's partner homeschooling, this questionnaire would be used to match partnered homeschool families.

Some questions it would include are the following: Would your partner homeschool prefer days, afternoons, evenings, midnights, or some combination of these hours? What age is your child or children? Has the parent who intends to be a teacher graduated from high school? What position do you desire in the partner homeschool? Would you say the general activity level of your child or children is very active, active, average, not so active, or very inactive?

Also include by multiple choice or written reply some hobbies, sports, arts, and other interests enjoyed by the families. As the questionnaires come in, the contact enters them into a matching program on the computer. (Look, I've created some jobs!)

The program will match geographic proximity as first priority, hours that work best second, and activity levels third. If there are many partnered homeschools in one geographic proximity, the hobbies, sports, arts, and other interests could take fourth. These are mainly included to further match within activity levels. The ultimate geographic proximity would be neighbors that match, next those that match within walking distance, and then those who may need to drive or be bused.

Yes, some jobs may be lost or changed. However, less buses will be better for the environment and save school districts money. Not heating, lighting, or cleaning elementary school buildings will do the same. This is why the principal would be most likely to administer the partner homeschool program. Partner homeschool teachers would be expected to teach in their best hours.

I am trying to provide as much flexibility as possible to the partner homeschools because the system is also to build better communities and closer families as well as educate our children! You might have realized one parent would be staying "home" and partner homeschooling while the other parent works? If not, well, they do unless it's a single parent household.

For further explanation, let's use the two parent household. The working parent's hours of work should be considered when choosing best hours especially for the teachers as this is where the partner homeschool will be located- the teacher's house.

If the working parent works days then traditional school hours would possibly be best. Likewise, if the working parent works midnights then afternoon, evening, or midnight hours would be best depending on when the working parent sleeps.

In my experiences and observations, the children often prefer to sleep when their parents sleep and be up when their parents are up. Having worked mainly afternoons and midnights, I slept days. I have more energy on afternoons and midnights. School from 8:00am to 3:00pm never really worked for me. Three of my four children were also afternoons and midnights almost from birth! Matching by best hours helps ensure more time for family togetherness and mental alertness. It's proven we learn better when more mentally alert as well.

The best hours will also likely tie-in with activity levels. Kids with ADHD would probably be in the extremely high activity level. They could be more easily set down, without medicating, after active learning or with the promise of active learning as a reward after completing sit-down learning. Traditionally, public schools have been sit-down learning. Active learning would be an example of where the interests from the questionnaire plays a greater part in matching. In fact, the interests should be added within the activity level matching.

For example: The extremely energetic teacher is also interested in basketball and soccer. He or she would be matched with extreme energy children who are interested in basketball or soccer. Both require the higher activity level. The middle activity levels, as you might guess, have the greater possibilities for matching. On the extremely low activity level, many of the children are likely disabled. Interests in video gaming and computers may be better matches as well as other lower activity level interests. Some other lower activity examples may be crocheting, knitting, playing cards or board games, archery, and bowling. So by matching interests within energy levels, we honor the children and help them learn in their best way possible!

I think some of you might be screaming at the video game match? Well, from personal experience, I can tell you they take a lot more strength, energy, and coordination than they're given credit for! Also, why all the simulators in training our Armed Services? Playing games and being at the computer for longer and longer periods of time has restrengthened my shoulder, forearm, and hands more than the more expensive physical therapy ever did! To play the game, you have to concentrate and plan moves. Putting the mind on the game takes it off the pain until the pain hits a level the

mind can no longer ignore.
For me, after awhile, I
didn't feel the pain until
the next day. Then of
course, I had more of a down
day.

After the matching is
done, the contact would send
a letter to each partner
homeschool teacher
introducing the other matched
families. Basically, this is
the teacher's class list.
However, it should be a
pretty short list. The
partner homeschools would
also have parents matched by
cooks, caregivers, and
cleaners. These are support
parents to the teacher. They
allow the teacher to
concentrate on teaching. I'm
going to explain the partner
homeschool set-up more, but
ask you to keep in mind the
"love not force"
implementation. Meaning in
part, that if the teachers
and supports have a way that
works better for them and the
children then they have the
flexibility to do it. My
ideas for the basic duties of
each are as follows.

The teacher does what teachers in public schools have traditionally done. They plan the lessons, teach them, correct them, and record them. They also choose the curriculum they feel is best for them and other families in their partner homeschool. The core curriculum must be reading, writing, spelling, math, science, and history. Reading, writing, spelling, and math taught on a daily basis with science and history more flexible. I taught two weeks of history or science in alternating weeks. My girls seemed to remember more, thereby learned more, by concentrating on one or the other.

Caregivers support the teacher by taking care of the younger children and giving the teacher a break if needed. They provide "recess". Other supports are welcome to help when not performing their duties of course. Caregivers also plan activities for the younger children. Playing house, painting, doing Lego building, and whatever else is age appropriate and within interests and activity levels. Caregivers are technically teachers for the younger children.

Cooks cook of course! LOL OK, they plan meals, buy the food needed for their planned meals, and make them. Since cooks sign-up to be cooks, it is believed they at least enjoy cooking. They also need to be versed in healthy eating or should learn. Other supports can and are encouraged to make suggestions for meals.

I would like to point out that this partner homeschool cooking eliminates school lunches and expenses. Children will be eating healthier. Also, we would lower illness within the community because we're not putting large crowds of children together to pass it around. Please note as well, public school cooks would not necessarily lose their jobs as they can sign-up to be partner homeschool cooks or move to other cooking positions within the high school or community.

Cleaners support the teacher by keeping the teacher's house clean. They clean bathrooms, dust, vacuum, sweep, and mop as needed. They also do the dishes after meals. However, the cook should clean the stove and food preparation areas.

That's the basic partner homeschool set-up. It would be hoped that the teacher and his or her supports would be matched so well that they not only work together educating our children, but become close friends within the community. This would strengthen our communities too! Stronger, closer communities have been shown by researchers to have lower crime rates. At the very least, the partner homeschool children have four adults to bond with instead of just

one. Not only that, but they
aren't sharing the bond and
attention with 15 to 35 other
children. Each teacher is
only assigned up to six
children!

As the younger children
grow to school age,
caregivers can become
teachers within their partner
homeschool. They may also
sign-up as teachers with
their already matched and
bonded children. They may
wish to remain caregivers but
start over instead.
Remember, love and choice!

Some other supports would
be available to partner
homeschool families. These
would be "Traveling Teachers"
and shared finances. As you
might guess, Traveling
Teachers go into the
partnered homeschools and
help the partner homeschool
teacher. This would be by
request of the teacher or any
of the other adults in the
partner homeschool.
Depending on the partner
homeschool area, Traveling
Teachers may be assigned to

partner homeschools at the beginning of the year.

For example: A small town may have six partner homeschools and only one or two Traveling Teachers. Names and phone numbers would be given to the one or two Traveling Teachers for all six partner homeschools. On the flipside, large cities like Chicago for example, would have a Traveling Teacher assigned by area of residence to the partnered homeschools.

Again, these assignments would be made with neighbors being the first choice. Walking distance would be the second choice. Then driving distance would be the third choice. Each Traveling Teacher would be assigned to a suggested six to ten partner homeschools. Local districts will decide how many partner homeschools to assign each Traveling Teacher.

I would recommend keeping the numbers lower and adding more Traveling Teachers to

the area district if needed.
I think I just created jobs
for more teachers? A class
of 35 students has one
teacher, but 35 students
could have many partner
homeschools with six children
in various locations.
Therefore, the district would
need at least two Traveling
Teachers. More would be
assigned as needed per
location as already
discussed. Each grade would
likely need at least two
Traveling Teachers as well.
This scenario doubles the
number of teachers needed!
Traveling Teachers could also
have general over sight of
their partner homeschools IF
local voters vote to do so.
General over sight would also
be defined by LOCAL VOTERS!

However, since it's my
idea, I would suggest that
the general over sight would
be limited to collecting
partner homeschool teachers'
grading records which would
help the Traveling Teacher
know where the partner
homeschool needs more
assistance, help choosing

curriculum, and possibly a test given by the Traveling Teachers at the beginning and end of each year to assess learning of the children. This test would be made by the local district and used to help partnered homeschools and Traveling Teachers to improve their children's learning. It would NOT be used to end a partnered homeschool except in extreme circumstances!

Even if extreme circumstances seem to exist, before a partner homeschool could be ended and the children reassigned to another partner homeschool, the one in question would appear before the local school board at a stated and regular meeting for review. Then by secret ballot all present, and ONLY all present at that meeting, would vote yes or no to end the partner homeschool in question. If the vote ties or is less than 60%-40% in favor of ending the partner homeschool then it shall continue on with greater help and supervision until the next test when another assessment is done. Hopefully, with greater help the partner homeschool will improve enough not to need another board review and vote. A struggling partner homeschool could request a permanent Traveling Teacher be assigned to do their teaching as well. Again, remember, the nonforce, love rule!

I also wrote about a financial partnership. Partner homeschools would attend all district head counts. The per pupil funding would be divided in half. Half goes to the district to provide Traveling Teachers and administration. The other half goes to the partner homeschools to pay for curriculum and provide income to the partner homeschool teachers and supports.

For example: If the district gets $6,000 per pupil, the district keeps $3,000 per pupil. The partnered homeschool gets

$3,000 per pupil as well.
That means a partnered
homeschool with six children
would get $18,000. The
partner homeschool teacher
chooses a $1,000 curriculum
so $17,000 would be divided
evenly among the supports as
pay or income.

However, the partnered
homeschool may wish to save
some portion as well. Since
some meals will be cooked at
the teacher's home, other
families may feel savings for
this to be appropriate.
Supplies like scissors, glue,
rulers, and paper that need
replenishing would be paid
for out of the savings.
Also, the teacher will likely
have some added expenses for
utility bills and home
repairs and maintenance.
There may be other needs of
the partner homeschool as
determined by the partner
homeschool teacher and
supports. The teacher and
supports should decide how
these items will be paid for
or dealt with before any
money is paid out. Again, I
have created more jobs,

gotten more money in circulation which increases buying power and tax revenue, and provided families more time together with children to have more bonding opportunity. This makes a stronger, happier, healthier community and life for all!

As I wrote before, we need to open a conversation about the middle school years. On further thinking, I would be inclined to send all partner homeschool children to a private or public school. My reasoning comes more from my idea for high school than from the partner homeschool idea. Middle schools would be "traditional" though various hours beyond the traditional could be offered. The traditional 8:00/8:30am-3:00/3:30pm would definitely be available. However, I would also suggest other shifts be available in the middle schools as well as the high schools. (Look, we need more teachers and principals for the other shifts! I created more jobs again.)

The local district would set the shifts available based on the partner homeschools. If most partner homeschools were actually on days and afternoons, it would make sense to have day and afternoon shifts. Possible shifts being traditional hours and maybe a shift starting at 1:00/1:30pm and ending at 8:00/8:30pm. If for some reason most partner homeschools were afternoons and midnights then the traditional hours might make sense to be dropped. Instead, possibly offer 3:00/3:30pm to 10:00/10:30pm and 11:00/11:30pm to 6:00/6:30am hours.

Some other jobs that may be affected by these ideas are bus drivers and kitchen or meal jobs. Buses and bus drivers as well as kitchen or meal jobs are added here too. It may not be buses, but some sort of free student transportation is to be provided for partner homeschools if needed in rural areas and definitely

for middle and high school
students. Funding that used
to go to elementary building
utilities, cleaning, and
maintenance could be
redirected to pay for this.

Middle school students
would sign-up for their hours
while in fifth grade. I'm
sorry; I don't remember when
signing-up is usually done!
However, it would be done
early enough for the district
to plan and get things in
order for the next year. The
middle school students would
not yet have class choices.
They would have state
requirements for sure. They
might also have federal
requirements. I lean toward
no federal requirements
beyond allowing partner
homeschools as explained;
free to the student
transportation; middle and
high school availability; and
funding from the feds to the
states.

State education
requirements would most
likely be traditional with
reading, writing, spelling,

vocabulary building (Language Arts), math strengthening with at least beginning algebra in eighth grade, science, history, computing, and gym with health classes. Band, art, woodworking, metal working, home economics, small engine repair, and other such types of classes could fill the day. Middle school students would then have their choice of one class. I suggest band and art be required offerings as these classes not only enrich the student's life, but open future employment opportunities on a much wider scale than other choices. Band and art also provide greater fall-back and supplemental income opportunities.

By the time students reach high school, they should have solid skills in the basics! However, I would recommend continuing them for practice and memory sake. Through-out the partner homeschool years and middle school years observations of each students' likes and dislikes as well as strengths and weaknesses should be made by the partner homeschool teachers and supports, Traveling Teachers, and Middle School Teachers and staff. These observations will be used to help High School Counselors, students, and the students' parents make initial career plans. Courses taken in high school beyond math, language arts, and government should be chosen by the initial career chosen. College is not for everyone!

Some people might want to be farmers, bakers, woodworkers, or metal workers for example. These career paths could "go back to the olden days" and give high school students on-the-job training or internships. Communities might build Career Centers to train for these types of jobs. Big Rapids, Michigan used to have a regional career center. Each community should decide what would work best for them to prosper in. Colleges and universities could offer

these classes too. However,
I would suggest dropping the
"baloney requirements of the
first two years"!

Continue offering Dual
Enrollment especially for
those students on a career
path that requires college or
university. High School
should stay somewhat
traditional in sports, band,
and art. I gave reasons for
this previously. It also
gives our young adults more
community time than family
time which is a major part of
growing up at about the right
time in their lives according
to many psychologists and
developmental experts. I
believe with stronger
families, stronger
communities, and stronger
transitional living; we will
have less trouble with ills
of society and more peace,
love, and prosperity.

Before I leave the
education topic, some words
to higher institutes of
learning. Instead of the
"baloney requirements of the
first two years" as mentioned

before, go right into the
needed studies for the
careers. Stop the big
business rip-offs! For
doctors, start them as
traditional as many times
they won't likely have enough
biology, chemistry, or
physics in high school.
However, they still should
not need the "baloney
requirements". "Baloney
requirements" are English and
social science as well as
math. I like the Freshman
Adjustment Class that I've
heard about in some colleges
and universities. All
Freshman should be required
to take such a class at the
BEGINNING of their Freshman
year!

Then again, maybe
students on a college or
university career path should
have such a class required in
their Senior year of high
school? Many of them cover
having a roommate(s), time
management, peer pressures of
college, and study habits.
If given in high school,
community resources and
college or university

financing could be covered
more extensively than it
currently is in one night.
Also, applying for college or
university could be part of
the class as well as what to
look for in each and how to
pick a college or university.
Education is important! A
GOOD education helps our kids
grow into knowledgeable,
happy, loving, confident,
prosperous adults.

7 HEALTH CARE

Again, I'm trying to keep my ideas timeless. However, I'm writing this at a time that Obamacare is still in effect as well as hold a belief that health care needs change sometimes frequently and sometimes over long periods of time. Obamacare is more easily dealt with. Repeal it and restore the old way. Then make a few changes to the old way.

Please keep in mind that earlier in this book I explained a company's "health" or "value" would depend on hourly salary, bonuses, and benefits paid, given to their employees. Health Insurance would be one of those valuable benefits. This would encourage companies to pay for employee's health insurance. Also, restore other laws that were changed or included in Obamacare under the guise of health care- for example the 40 hour work week which was lowered to 30 hours!

Changes to the old way were included in Obamacare and were all that I believe would have been necessary at the time! Those changes are:

1. No lifetime caps.
2. No preexisting condition exclusions.
3. Keep children on their parents' insurance policies until they're 26. I would add to that however! I would add: unless they marry, become parents themselves, or are employed by a company that provides insurance to their employees.
4. Expand Medicaid to persons in poverty. I remind you of my idea to have doctors pay back student loans by having 10% of their patients on Medicaid and charging it against their loans. This helps keep Medicaid costs down and should allow for the continued expansion. Also, ALL states would expand under the same poverty law(s)!

I would suggest seeing how these changes work out. After that, I might consider regulating the insurance companies further to keep costs, deductibles, and copays down. Maybe with these changes, doctors can charge way less as well? Eight hundred dollars per hour for a doctor is shameful. Yes, $800/hr is what I said! As well is anything over $100/hr I hazard to say.

That leads me to mention Tort Reform. No amount of money will bring back a loved one! Doctors make mistakes and stuff just happens. When someone dies wrongfully, have the doctor's insurance pay for the burial plus $200,000 divided to the patient's beneficiary or beneficiaries- parents or guardians if a child; spouse and children if an adult. A mark would then be put on the doctor's record. The doctor will undergo a review by doctors in the same field, but associated with different hospitals. Maybe even make that doctors in the same field and 100 or more miles from the doctor being reviewed. The reviewing doctors will decide if the marked doctor can continue practicing fully licensed, on restricted license, or lose his/her license. This will happen after every mark and all previous marks are reviewed at all reviews. Upon review, the insurance company must provide reviewing doctors with all previous marks and explanations.

If the patient doesn't die, but has ongoing health impairment or needs, the doctor's insurance will pay the patient's continued health care and mark the doctor's record. A review would then be done as explained above. An amount up to one year of the patient's wages would be paid to the patient as well. If the patient is a child then up to one year's wages of the highest earning parent's or guardian's wages would be paid by the doctor's insurance to the parent(s) or guardian(s).

These laws should help keep the doctor's insurance rates down and therefore doctor's charges down. Yet, it does provide some relief for the patient and their family as well as consequence and policing of doctors. Other health care and tort reform must be brought up or requested as needed over time. However, I believe I have written a good start.

8 A WORD ABOUT DRUGS

Legalize all drugs! Part of my reasoning comes from my belief, knowledge, and teachings about medicines. The main belief is that ALL medicines can become drugs! When medicines are taken wrong, not as prescribed, and/or abused, they no longer heal and often hurt patients like drugs. People who use or do drugs are often in need of medicine. They should not be put in prison. Instead, they should feel free to seek and receive treatment. Many who use drugs are mentally ill.

Likewise, we as a society should consider using, doing drugs disgraceful. Drugs hurt people and destroy families and communities. They are NOT cool! By decriminalizing drugs and prescribing them if needed for awhile in treatment, the drug dealers and cartels are more likely to go away as large amounts of money for drugs won't be available.

This will probably lower crime rates too.

As a society, we need to teach our children to be healthy. We need to teach the difference between medicine and drugs. We need to know and understand as adults that not all medicines work the same way in all people. What is medicine to one person is a drug to another!

Alcohol and marijuana are very good examples of this. Some people can enjoy one or two drinks and be just fine. Someone else may get drunk on the same two drinks. One person may drink a whole six pack of beer, be a little loud or obnoxious, and be just fine the next day. Another person may drink one beer and have a horrible headache the next day. The person with the horrible headache may be sensitive or allergic to one or more ingredients of the beer. Even prescribed medicines act differently in different people.

This acting differently in different people is a main reason I highly disagree that marijuana never hurts anyone and is totally safe! That is NOT true in my experience of watching and knowing marijuana users. It is definitely not what society should be teaching its children about it! Some people who use marijuana just lay around and do nothing or eat a lot. Some people get very anxious, paranoid, or both. Sometimes their paranoia leads them to abuse people around them or commit other crimes.

Though it seems very rare that other crimes besides abuse are committed. Some people DO toke and drive as well. Driving while high, drunk, buzzed, or even influenced by medicinal side effects is VERY dangerous! This is what society should also teach the children. Those situations should be illegal. However, consequences of driving influenced by medicinal side effects should be more lenient as the person may not have known how the medicine influenced them. Medicinal influence can change suddenly as well.

Again, legalize drugs! Make them available through prescription. I guess that means turn them into the possible medicines they could be for some people. Educate our children about medicines verses drugs. Make appropriate protection laws such as no driving while buzzed, drunk, high, or under the influence in any way. No smoking anything neither in public nor around children. Second hand smoke and buzzes or highs affect people differently as well.

Since smoke spreads without bounds, people who choose not to smoke or toke need protection laws. Maybe smokers could build detached smoking sheds in their backyards? A smoking place where the smoke does not even seep back into the house, apartment, or whatever living space. If you don't have

children or a non-smoker to
consider, you can smoke in
your living space as long as
it is not attached to another
person's living space such as
they are in apartment
buildings, duplexes, and
triplexes.

I think some background on my beliefs and studies in biology to become a veterinarian will help you understand what I believe about abortion. The debated question of "When does life begin?" has been argued for centuries and will probably be argued for many more regardless of what I write here! Maybe what I write will lessen or clarify the argument some? My main belief is we as a society should prevent unwanted pregnancies and make life better for people as a whole so the reasons women choose abortion go down or go away altogether. Society has made great improvement in my life time. Keep working on it!

That's one part of the solution. The other is the actual question of "When does life begin?" POTENTIAL for life begins when a male and a female have sex, make-love, or whatever term you use for the penis entering the vagina. This potential exists even when steps have been taken to prevent a pregnancy. However, it is ONLY a potential! Once this potential exists, then the next potential exists. The potential of an egg meeting a sperm and becoming fertilized.

Even if this happens, many cell divisions must take place. Life has not begun which is why the "morning after pill" is not an abortion pill. It makes an unacceptable environment. It should not be used regularly as contraception though because it has dangerous side effects. Anyway, back to the process of becoming pregnant.

Once the egg and sperm cells meet and divide, they still must imbed in the uterus. It is then that the growth process speeds up to become a fetus. However, it is still only a potential for life. Now a greater potential than before, but still only a potential. Cell divisions continue even after

the joined egg,sperm cell
imbeds into the uterus.

Once imbedded into the
uterus, the organs begin to
form. The brain and spine
are first to form. By the
female's second missed
menstrual cycle, the fetus is
now a complete baby if all
has grown and developed as it
should. This is about eight
weeks from the last menstrual
cycle. I still say there is
only potential for life as
the baby cannot under
"normal" circumstances
survive outside of the
mother. However, it's this
knowledge we need to teach as
it adds, at least in my
belief, the greater moral,
mental, and emotional
questions to the debate.
Knowing that the baby is
there and complete by eight
weeks, can you still desire
the abortion? Some can; some
cannot.

Of course, the potential
for life outside of the
mother continues to grow for
the next nine months. Please
note I added "outside of the

mother". I do believe the potential for life is so much greater after the eighth week that life has begun. By the eighth week, pregnancy can usually be confirmed and a whole baby is living in the Mother's uterus. Again, knowing the whole baby is there growing and developing, can you still go through with an abortion at nine or more weeks? I repeat. Some can; some can't.

It is more of a moral, mental, and emotional issue. Some can because they may have been raped. Some can because they can't mentally or emotionally live with the idea of adoption. These are two reasons women still choose abortion. There are many more. Although to me, abortion is not the issue; UNWANTED pregnancy is. Unwanted pregnancy is heartbreaking!

However, I'm writing about abortion policy and when life begins. Until the baby is born and takes its first breath outside of the

Mother, I believe it's still only potential for life- greater and greater potential. Since many miscarriages happen in the first twelve weeks, abortion should be or remain legal for the first twelve weeks. Possibly to the fifteenth week as some women don't know they're pregnant until the twelfth week.

Mid-term and late-term abortions should remain legal between the Mother and her doctor, but not at abortion clinics. Mid-term and late- term would preferably only happen when the Mother's life is in danger, the baby will be so unhealthy as to have a bad life, or both. These are mentally and emotionally heartbreaking situations! As a loving society, we should not judge. Again, love not force!

So yes, I'm pro-choice AND pro-life on abortion! I believe in education and preventing unwanted pregnancies. I believe in a loving society that encourages females to have their babies. A loving society to support and develop every life that is born to reach health, happiness, prosperity, and love! Naive? Maybe! Dreaming? Definitely! Won't you dream with me and strive to make our dream come true?

10 MARRIAGE

Notice I did not say, "Same-sex Marriage" nor "Marriage Equality". The reason is the Federal Government needs to define marriage as this:

For the purpose of law and its enforcement, marriage is defined as between two and only two consenting adults. (Adults being the age one is considered lawfully an adult which is usually 18 years old at this time.)

Please let me explain my reasoning! To keep polygamists and bisexuals reading as well, let us address their issues first. You will probably figure out some of my further explanation as well. Polygamists and bisexuals can still be polygamists and bisexuals. However, only the first marriage will be legally recognized by government entities. Polygamists to my knowledge have a hierarchy to their wives. The government will stay out of that religious debate as per the 1st Amendment to the Constitution. Also, to my knowledge, bisexuals often look at both sexes when seeking a mate. However, they usually fall in love with or grow to love someone and commit to that one. Yet, there are some bisexuals who need or have one of each and desire to commit to two people. The government will allow the two marriages, but recognize only the first marriage under the law.

My further reasoning includes some history. Way back history includes many polygamists. King David anyone? I'm not really sure when marriage became between two people and between a man and a woman. It's basically irrelevant except from the religious and lawful debate. Religiously, most churches believed or came to believe that marriage was to be between one man and one woman. Most churches performed marriages in this manner until about the

1990's. It's only recently
then that some churches
started marrying two
consenting adults of the same
sex. Many of these marriages
were in churches with
"freedom" doctrines. These
churches have long been
recognized by the government
as established religions and
churches. This establishes a
religious acceptance to same
sex marriage.

Historically, our
government has recognized
marriages performed in the
church. The government has
also performed non-religious
marriages in city halls and
recognized these. Therefore,
if churches are now accepting
and performing marriages
between two consenting same
sex adults, our government
MUST legally recognize these
marriages under continuity of
the 1st Amendment to the
Constitution. The
government's alternative
would be to no longer
recognize nor perform any
marriage. I suspect many
readers do not want our
government to no longer

perform nor recognize marriage. Again, give others freedom so you can have or keep freedom! Under this explanation and upholding the Constitution of the United States of America, I believe this definition of marriage is correct, acceptable, and ends the debate. This definition provides for freedom and greater happiness. Love not force!

There are benefits of marriage provided between a man and a woman. With my definition, these benefits would go to the two consenting adults. It will also stop abuse of marriage. It will stop some assistance and Social Security fraud. In this instance, a Federal definition of marriage as stated, would trump the states as it gives more freedom to We the People. This is the intended separation of power between the Federal and State Governments as well. States can give MORE freedom than the Federal Government, but NOT less! Again, I argue the

1st Amendment and historical
recognition of marriage to
support the definition of
marriage presented.

I reiterate by belief in the Constitution of the United States of America. It's not perfect, but it is an excellent start. It has allowed and helped America to live in greater peace and prosperity for hundreds of years. Americans have had greater freedom than many other countries as well. The United States has had its growing pains and will likely continue to have them. However, the Constitution when upheld and improved in the spirit of "Life, Liberty, and the Pursuit of Happiness" lends great guidance for government and life. I recommend it for all countries!

This of course would mean learning the Constitution of the United States of America. It means learning to live under its guidance. Sometimes living under it means agreeing to disagree. Sometimes it means ignoring things you don't like or don't believe in because

someone else does. It often
means lovingly giving freedom
to another so you keep your
freedom as well.

Of course, I would
recommend the changes I have
written about earlier in this
book for the reasons I've
written! Many times I've
written "Love not force!"
Learn to talk about problems
and work them out. War makes
me SO SAD:(:(It destroys
families! It causes pain for
families, friends, and loved
ones! War and killing should
be avoided at all costs!

Another thing sad about
war is all the lost beauty
and heritage of the countries
doing the fighting. I admit
Canada is the only country
I've gone to outside of the
United States. However, I'm
an infamous "arm chair
traveler"! I love looking at
pictures of other countries
and talking on the internet
to people who live there.
Before the recent wars in
Egypt and Syria, I thought
both countries had beautiful
buildings, beautiful cities,

and beautiful country sides
and land. Now I see pictures
and cry because so much of
the beauty is gone:(The
heritage of old beauty,
standing stories of the past
gone. Destroyed! It's so
wrong and so sad:(:(

Instead, let's live in
peace and prosperity!
Preserve the beauty of the
past! Make every country a
place others want to visit.
A place others feel safe and
are safe visiting. Charge
sales tax (VAT tax)to help
financially support the
country. Continue living in
your country and work to make
it better. If someone sends
you an e-mail, text, or other
message then think if it's
real or not. Think if what
they said would be good for
your country. Does it
peacefully promote change?
Does the change make greater
freedom? Does the change
create more prosperity? Will
the change make the city,
country, town, village more
livable, more beautiful, or
both?

If yes then work to make the change happen. Ask family and friends if they agree with you and would help you. If no then maybe think of a way to better the idea so the answers become yes or just throw the whole idea out. If it promotes war, destruction, pain, and sadness; throw it out! Again, peace, love, and prosperity- not force!

I would also suggest a world wide minimum wage. I'm not sure how this would be implemented at this time. I do know it's needed along with other truly fair trade practices. I believe others have more ideas on this, but needed to mention the beginning of them here. These ideas are important!

Basically, everyone accepts responsibility for their own country. Everyone works to make their own country what they want it to be through peaceful means. I'm willing to continue teaching and talking as I desire very much to make the world a better place through this book as well as the rest of my life. We all need to help each other. We were all born on Earth to live on Earth. Life is always evolving; always changing; it is never ending! How do you want life to be for you? Your family? Your friends? Your country? Make it so!

If it would help to offer yearly awards to countries, we could do that too. Maybe awards for highest paid employees, best customer services, safest, happiest, and most peaceful could be some examples. Awards could be with trophies and/or monetary possibly through the United Nations. Whatever helps make a lasting, loving, peaceful world.

12 TV IDEA- STRENGTHENING "WE THE PEOPLE"

This chapter and the idea it contains is copied from my e-mail which was originally sent on June 13, 2010. I had e-mailed it to a local television station. After some months, they denied acceptance of my idea by claiming a lack of time and money. If after I put this here and anyone but the President of the United States or I runs the debate, I claim copyright and royalties. If the President runs it, so be it. If I run it, I get paid as negotiated.

It would be a debate show which would give the people one week to vote on the question or law of the week. At which time, the final vote would be announced at the beginning of each show. Afterwards, it would be forwarded to Congress. Each show I would debate BOTH sides of the issue or question with a "leader" or guest from each side. I would debate them one at a time.

If 65% of the people vote for the question or law, it becomes law until it comes up for vote again. Issues or questions can only come up once a year. No law could be passed without this "more than the majority vote". We would possibly have to make this the first issue or question? If passed then it would go into an annotated law book.

Each part of the health care bill could have been done this way for example. Once the "No exemption for pre-existing conditions" passed, it would go into the annotated Health Care Laws. Each law book would then be kept by the appropriate government agency. Of course, this would be for domestic issues or laws only; at least at this time. This would leave the President and Congress more time to tend to world issues.

Part of this idea and my belief that it would be a successful show comes from already successful reality TV shows who have had MILLIONS voting on their shows. I originally gave specific titles to these shows, but changed this to be more generic and timeless. Many more reality TV shows now exist as well. If the show's issues or questions will become law with the 65% majority, people will be more likely to watch and vote?!

I believe this would solve the problem I've heard from many through the years in online chats as well. People want change, but feel powerless to make it happen. Myself included! I think this could be a way to re-empower the people. I desire to be a leader in this empowerment and am asking you/your station to be co-leaders for empowerment and change- "of the people, by the people, and for the people".

13 ENDING

It's long past time for
WE THE PEOPLE to UNITE for
Love and prosperity! UNITE
and prosper for ourselves,
for the United States of
America, and for the world.
Remember, "United we stand;
divided we fall"!

We are not a bunch of
evil sinners. We are GOOD.
We are LOVE. We are Life. We
are manKIND. We are US-
United States, United
Standing- WE THE PEOPLE-
finally, finally awake,
loving, and UNITED for Love
and Life-

I finish with a pledge for
        "US"...

14 A PLEDGE FOR THE WORLD

We are One World,
One race- ManKIND(ManKIND)
United by Love
Dedicated to living, creating
lives of happiness, peace,
justice, and charity
        to all:)

ABOUT THE AUTHOR

RainBlue owns Rain's Realm LLC which has not had its "brick and mortar" home yet. She shares her real name with an already published author, photographer, and social activist! This and the fact that she has been online chatting and posting since 1993 mostly under the nick RainBlue is the reason she published under this pen name. Since using the nick, she has learned that Rain stands for "Life giver or teacher" and Blue for "Healer" among Native American and spiritual cultures. She feels the nick is perfect for her!

She is also a very proud Mother and Grandmother! She has numerous interests and hobbies as well as a deep desire to make the world a better place to live for many generations; even all time. She lives in the extremely beautiful Upper Peninsula of Michigan in the United States of America.